MARQUES J. C

REINVENTION

SIMPLE ACTIONS FOR ACHIEVING SUCCESS

BLACK AND WHITE EDITION

Clark**House**

PUBLISHING

REINVENTION: Simple Actions for Achieving Success

Copyright © 2020 by Marques J. Clark.

All rights reserved. Printed in the United States of America. Aurora, Illinois. No part of this book may be used or reproduced in any manner whatsoever without the prior written permission of the copyright owner except in the case of brief quotations embodied in critical articles and reviews.

Photography Marques J. Clark.

Cover photo by Kyndall Clark.

Library of Congress Control Number: 2020900501

ISBN 978-1-7344714-0-3 (Black and White Edition)

ISBN 978-1-7344714-2-7 (Color Edition)

ISBN 978-1-7344714-1-0 (e-book)

FIRST EDITION

ClarkHouse Publishing, LLC books may be purchased for educational, business, or sales promotional use. Special editions or book excerpts can also be created to specification. For more information, please email mclark@clarkhousepublishing.com.

ClarkHouse
PUBLISHING

For Noah and Micah

This book is dedicated to your future self. You are about to embark on a journey that will unlock your personal power and give you access to opportunities. May you be rewarded with success, happiness, and wealth for making the choice to invest in yourself.

CONTENTS

AUTHOR'S NOTE

We are all on a journey to become the greatest version of ourselves, but sometimes, our journey is not what we expect it to be. Sometimes, it is filled with failure, disappointment, unmet expectations, and negative opinions. Each day, we are given the chance to be better than we were yesterday, but our insecurities trick us into believing that we cannot become the person we desire to be.

We tell ourselves that we are not good enough for *this* opportunity, that we cannot accomplish *that* goal, or that we are not smart enough to compete with everyone else. As I was writing this book I could hear a voice in my head: "Who do you think you are? You can't write a book. Stop before you embarrass yourself!" The constant lies we tell ourselves prevent us from reaching our true potential.

I wrote REINVENTION to remind myself, as well as others, to stop believing those lies. There are no limitations to what can be achieved. The person you want to be is inside you, waiting to be let out. The only way to do that is by remembering to wear your crown – a symbol for your confidence, your power, and your ability to always believe in yourself.

PREFACE

I've made thousands of mistakes, I've struggled more times than I can count, and I've failed, over and over again. Many of my failures were a result of me not having any guidance on what I *should* be doing to navigate life successfully.

In the African American community, we don't spend a lot of time discussing topics like mental health, relationship building, achieving goals, or generational wealth. The media often portrays negative stereotypes of African American men. Those same stereotypes affected how I felt about myself and how I defined success. As a teenager, I wanted to become successful and make a lot of money, but the *only* images I saw of successful African American millionaires were athletes, entertainers, or drug dealers. I didn't have any special athletic abilities, I couldn't sing, rap, or play an instrument, and selling drugs...it just wasn't an option for me. I had to find another way.

School doesn't teach you the life lessons you need to become successful, and our parents don't always have the answers; trying to figure out where to start can be frustrating. Because of *my* lack of information, I continued to struggle and make many mistakes. I reached a point in my life where failure became the norm for me, and over time, I stopped believing in myself. After going through depression and feeling defeated for so long, I finally worked up enough courage to make a change; I began asking for help.

I wanted to find out how a person with no money, no connections, and no opportunities could *still* manage to become successful, despite barriers. For three years, I interviewed and studied over 100 highly successful men, including entrepreneurs, investors, multi-millionaires, philanthropists, educators, public speakers, and CEOs. These men came from different backgrounds and various cultures but had one thing in common: they created their own success with very little resources. The most shocking part of it all? Each person achieved their success by making small changes in their life. No secrets or fancy strategies, just simple, but powerful, actions. In REINVENTION, you will learn what action you can take now that will guarantee your success for the future.

REINVENTION is not a novel. In fact, it is not your typical book at all. REINVENTION is written in a manner of speaking, filled with contractions, capitalizations, and informal grammar. REINVENTION is a lookbook. It features photos, graphics, large text, and various font styles. The photos featured in REINVENTION are images of young, professionally dressed, African American men - images that normally do not get highlighted by the media. Although REINVENTION is designed for young men who want to become successful, the easy-to-apply actions in this book can be utilized by anyone wanting to become a better version of themselves.

Seven themes were identified in my conversations with the successful men: self-awareness, resilience, gratitude, success habits, relationship building, financial literacy, and self-confidence. To get the most out of this book, I encourage you to do three things:

1. Read the entire book to understand each theme.
2. Apply the simple actions into your daily life, one by one.
3. If any of the actions resonate with you, stop reading and try them out. Yes, I want you to finish the book, but the progress you make on your success journey is far more important.

You define success, and only you. This is a concept that every successful person understands and lives by. By reading this book, you are making the choice to reach a new level of success by becoming a better version of yourself. Success begins with simply taking action. Believe you deserve more, be brave enough to demand more, and be disciplined enough to work for more.

-MJC

CHAPTER ONE

MIRRORS

*EVERYTHING YOU EXPERIENCE IS A REFLECTION OF **YOU**. YOUR REALITY MIRRORS YOUR BEHAVIOR. IN ORDER TO BE THE CHANGE YOU WANT TO SEE YOU MUST UNDERSTAND WHO YOU **TRULY** ARE.*

#SELF-AWARENESS

BELIEVING IN YOURSELF

IS THE HARDEST THING YOU'LL EVER HAVE TO DO,

BECAUSE THERE ARE SO MANY REASONS

WHY YOU *SHOULDN'T* DO IT.

YOUR MIND HAS BEEN

LYING TO YOU

– TRICKING YOU INTO BELIEVING
YOU'RE LESS THAN WHO YOU TRULY ARE:

———————————

"YOU CAN'T DO THAT."

"YOU'RE NOT GOOD ENOUGH."

"YOU'RE GOING TO FAIL."

"JUST GIVE UP."

———————————

AND YOU'VE BEEN LISTENING FOR SO LONG THAT
IT'S STARTING TO SOUND LIKE THE TRUTH:

———————————

"I CAN'T DO THAT."

"I'M NOT GOOD ENOUGH."

"IT WON'T WORK."

"I'LL NEVER BE ABLE TO..."

YOUR

WORST ENEMY

IS LIVING INSIDE
YOUR OWN HEAD

**– BLOCKING YOU FROM GREATER OPPORTUNITIES,
STOPPING YOU FROM ACCOMPLISHING YOUR GOALS,
AND PREVENTING YOU FROM ACHIEVING SUCCESS.**

INNER CRITIC

n. the negative voice in your head that judges and criticizes everything you do. It causes you to doubt your abilities, tricks you into lowering your expectations, and robs you of your confidence.

ONE OF THE

BIGGEST MISTAKES

WE MAKE IS

LISTENING TO OUR INNER CRITIC.

WE CREATE A FALSE REALITY IN OUR HEAD

BASED ON OUR FEARS AND OUR DOUBTS.

———————————

MOST PEOPLE DON'T REALIZE

HOW GREAT THEY TRULY ARE.

THEY LIVE THEIR WHOLE LIFE

PERFORMING BELOW THEIR POTENTIAL

AND NEVER ACHIEVE A <u>FRACTION</u> OF

WHAT THEY'RE ACTUALLY CAPABLE OF.

———————————

TO BECOME

THE GREATEST VERSION

OF YOURSELF, YOU MUST CONTROL YOUR INNER CRITIC.

YOU HAVE TO IDENTIFY NEGATIVE THOUGHTS AND

REMOVE YOUR LIMITING BELIEFS. YOU MUST

UNDERSTAND YOUR STRENGTHS AND

USE THEM TO YOUR ADVANTAGE.

YOU MUST LEARN YOUR

WEAKNESSES, THEN

IMPROVE THEM

OVER TIME.

YOU MUST RECOGNIZE YOUR REACTIONS, BEHAVIORS,

AND HABITS AS IF SOMEONE ELSE WAS OBSERVING YOU.

TO ACHIEVE SUCCESS, *YOU MUST*

INCREASE YOUR SELF-AWARENESS.

SELF-AWARENESS

IS OBSERVING YOUR THOUGHTS, FEELINGS,

BELIEFS, BEHAVIORS, STRENGTHS,

AND WEAKNESSES.

IT'S BEING HONEST WITH YOURSELF, AND

UNDERSTANDING

WHAT MAKES YOU THE PERSON YOU ARE.

HAVING SELF-AWARENESS GIVES YOU

CONFIDENCE

TO MAKE THE BEST CHOICES, AND THE ABILITY TO

CONTROL

HOW SUCCESSFUL YOU WILL BECOME.

DECISIONS ARE BEING MADE IN
YOUR LIFE RIGHT NOW.
THE QUESTION IS: ARE **YOU**
MAKING THE DECISIONS, OR IS
YOUR INNER CRITIC MAKING THEM
FOR YOU?

——

USE THE FOLLOWING SIMPLE
ACTIONS TO INCREASE YOUR
SELF-AWARENESS:

MONITOR YOUR INNER VOICE

We all have an inner voice that is saying positive or negative things inside our head. The way you talk to yourself can help you reach your potential, or prevent you from achieving success.

Pay attention to what your inner voice is saying and how it's making you feel.

Replace negative self-talk with positive self-talk.

Phrases like, "I can't," "I should be doing better," or, "I'm not good enough," limit your potential by making you feel bad about yourself – creating a negative attitude.

Positive self-talk makes you feel good about yourself and increases your confidence. Phrases like, "I can handle anything," or "I'm capable and confident," increases your self-esteem.

By monitoring your inner voice and replacing negative self-talk with positive self-talk, your confidence will increase, you'll become more optimistic and assertive when pursuing your dreams, and you'll have more control over your life.

EVALUATE YOUR THOUGHTS

USING A ONE-SENTENCE JOURNAL

Documenting your daily thoughts on paper, or electronically, will help you recognize patterns that could be harming you, or helping you achieve success.

Use these prompts and write one sentence a day:

What is going well in my life right now?

What could be going better in my life right now?

What can I accept that I can't change?

What is currently causing me the most stress?

What do I need to do that I keep putting off?

What is currently giving me the most joy?

What worries me the most about my future?

IDENTIFY YOUR
STRENGTHS AND WEAKNESSES

We all have strengths and weaknesses that make up who we are. Your weaknesses hold you back from reaching your potential, while your strengths help elevate you to your success.

On a piece of paper, or in your phone, make a list of your strengths and weaknesses. To help you think about what to include for your strengths and weaknesses, ask yourself these questions:

- What am I good at doing?
- What compliments have I received from other people?
- Which projects have I spent hours on without getting tired?
- What have others had to help me with on more than one occasion?
- What tasks and activities seem to drain my energy?

By identifying your strengths and weaknesses, you will be able to make the necessary improvements in your life that lead you directly to success.

ASK FOR FEEDBACK

FROM THE FIVE PEOPLE WHO KNOW YOU BEST

Receiving feedback allows you to see yourself as *others* see you – eliminating blind spots. Blind spots are characteristics that are seen by everyone except yourself.

Feedback gives you the power to identify and repair your challenges, and the confidence to use your strengths to your advantage.

Choose five people who know you well and ask them the following questions:

- What five words describe me the best?
- What do you appreciate most about our relationship?
- What is my greatest strength?
- What is something I can improve about myself?

Compare their responses to how you view yourself. What are the similarities? What are the differences? What surprised you about other people's feedback and why? How do opinions from friends and family members differ?

Don't let your
inner critic trick you
into believing that

AVERAGE

is the best you can do.

PRACTICE MEDITATION

Meditation is a technique used to control your mind and strengthen your mental health.

Not only does meditation increase your self-awareness, it reduces stress and anxiety, improves your sleep, increases your focus, helps to eliminate negative feelings, and gives you control of your thoughts.

Use the Headspace app to practice meditation.

Headspace is a mobile app that teaches you how to meditate by guiding you through each session. It's like having an instructor by your side for every step of your meditation journey, helping you become more aware.

Headspace tracks the sessions you complete so you can see how you've progressed over time. The app is free to download and comes with many free meditation sessions to get started. Once you feel like you've mastered the free sessions, you can choose to subscribe to get access to a library full of meditation exercises.

EVERY IDEA YOU IMAGINE, EVERY GOAL YOU SET,

AND EVERY DREAM YOU ENVISION

CAN BECOME YOUR REALITY.

NEVER UNDERESTIMATE YOUR

POWER.

YOUR MIND HAS THE POWER TO

TRANSFORM YOUR CURRENT CIRCUMSTANCES,

YOUR WORDS HAVE THE POWER TO

SPEAK THINGS INTO EXISTENCE,

AND YOUR ACTIONS HAVE THE POWER TO

CREATE THE SUCCESS YOU DESIRE.

YOU MUST FIRST MAKE THE CHOICE TO FULLY

BELIEVE IN YOURSELF.

CHAPTER TWO

STORMS

*THE CHALLENGES YOU FACE ARE
TEMPORARY SEASONS THAT ALWAYS PASS
WITH TIME. LEARNING TO OVERCOME
STORMS IN YOUR LIFE IS THE KEY THAT
WILL ELEVATE YOU TO SUCCESS.*

#RESILIENCE

WHEN LIFE IS GOOD EVERYTHING IS

BEAUTIFUL.

BUT WHEN YOU ENTER A
DIFFICULT SEASON,

LIFE CAN BRING PAIN.

DAYS TURN DARK AND GLOOMY, ONE BAD
EXPERIENCE SPIRALS INTO ANOTHER
HORRIFIC EVENT, AND BEFORE
YOU KNOW IT, YOU'RE
STUCK IN THE
MIDDLE
OF A

STORM.

STORMS

ARE THE OBSTACLES, CHALLENGES,

STRESSES, AND FAILURES

WE <u>ALL</u> FACE.

THEY'RE THE

INCONVENIENT, UNEXPECTED,

AND UNPREDICTABLE DISTURBANCES

THAT DISRUPT OUR LIVES, AND STAND

IN THE WAY OF

OUR HAPPINESS.

STORMS

FAILURE,
DEFEAT, BETRAYAL,
DISCRIMINATION, ABUSE,
VIOLENCE, BULLYING, ADDICTION,
DEPRESSION, JOB LOSS, SICKNESS, AND
DEATH ARE STORMS THAT CAUSE US TO LOSE
MOTIVATION, LOSE PATIENCE, AND LOSE OUR ABILITY TO

FACE THE FUTURE WITH FAITH.

SOMETIMES OUR STORMS GET THE BEST OF US.

NEGATIVE EVENTS MAY CAUSE US TO REACT IN WAYS WE NORMALLY WOULDN'T. WE BUILD WALLS TO BLOCK OUR PAIN, WE USE SUBSTANCES TO ESCAPE OUR STRESS, AND WE LET FEAR TRICK US INTO BELIEVING OUR SITUATION IS WORSE THAN IT APPEARS.

STORMS AFFECT
EVERYONE.

YOU

MIGHT

ASSUME

EVERYONE

ELSE IS LIVING

A STRESS-FREE LIFE.

THEY'RE NOT. THEY'RE MAKING

MISTAKES, THEY'RE FACING OBSTACLES,

THEY'RE DEALING WITH CHALLENGES, AND

THEY'RE EXPERIENCING DEFEAT, JUST LIKE YOU.

TO CONQUER THE
STORMS IN YOUR LIFE YOU MUST HAVE AN

INDESTRUCTIBLE
MINDSET.

YOU MUST EMBRACE CHANGE, OVERCOME OBSTACLES,
LEARN FROM YOUR MISTAKES, AND KEEP AN
OPTIMISTIC AND AMBITIOUS ATTITUDE.

TO ACHIEVE SUCCESS, *YOU MUST BUILD RESILIENCE.*

♛

RESILIENCE

IS YOUR ABILITY TO
OVERCOME SETBACKS IN YOUR LIFE.

IT'S THE MENTAL TOUGHNESS YOU HAVE INSIDE
YOU THAT ALLOWS YOU TO CONQUER
CHALLENGES AND BOUNCE BACK
FROM STRESSFUL SITUATIONS.

HAVING RESILIENCE
DOES NOT MEAN YOU WILL
STOP DEALING WITH DIFFICULTIES,
HAVING RESILIENCE MEANS YOU HAVE
ACCEPTED THAT STORMS ARE A PART OF LIFE
AND YOU'RE CHOOSING TO OVERCOME THEM.

HOW MANY MORE TIMES ARE YOU GOING TO DOUBT YOURSELF BEFORE YOU REALIZE YOU CAN MAKE IT THROUGH ANYTHING? YOUR TRACK RECORD FOR OVERCOMING DIFFICULTIES IS 100%. STOP SECOND-GUESSING WHAT YOU CAN DO. USE YOUR RESILIENCE.

EMBRACE FAILURE

AND ALLOW YOURSELF TO MAKE MISTAKES

DON'T ALLOW YOUR FEAR OF DEFEAT

TO OUTWEIGH YOUR

DESIRE TO SUCCEED.

FAILURE COMES BEFORE SUCCESS.

BEHIND EVERY SUCCESSFUL PERSON ARE <u>MANY</u>

UNSUCCESSFUL YEARS.

EXPECT AND ACCEPT SETBACKS.

YOU LEARN THE MOST WHEN YOU'RE

FACED WITH THE GREATEST CHALLENGES.

GIVE YOURSELF PERMISSION TO MAKE MISTAKES.

FORGIVE YOURSELF.

YOU'VE MESSED UP IN THE PAST AND YOU WILL

MESS UP AGAIN. EVERYONE MAKES MISTAKES,

AND EVERY SUCCESSFUL PERSON HAS FAILED.

YOU ARE NO DIFFERENT. NEVER PUNISH

YOURSELF FOR DOING SOMETHING

WRONG. INSTEAD, TAKE

ADVANTAGE OF THE

OPPORTUNITY

TO TRY

AGAIN.

WE BLAME OUR STRUGGLES FOR THE REASON WHY WE "CAN'T" BE GREAT BUT OUR STRUGGLES ARE THE REASON WHY WE WILL BECOME GREAT.

RESPOND TO SITUATIONS

INSTEAD OF REACTING TO THEM

WHEN YOU'RE DEALING WITH A

TOUGH SITUATION, IT MAY BE DIFFICULT

TO SEE A SOLUTION BECAUSE YOU'RE

TOO CLOSE TO THE PROBLEM.

ZOOM OUT.

FOCUS ON THE FACTS.

BEFORE ACTING ON IMPULSE,

BEFORE REACTING WITHOUT STRATEGIZING,

BEFORE MAKING A PERMANENT DECISION,

GIVE YOURSELF TIME TO THINK.

If you can't
CONTROL
what's happening to you,
control how you
RESPOND
to what's happening to you.

IF IT ISN'T GOING
TO MATTER IN

5 YEARS

DON'T SPEND MORE THAN

5 MINUTES

BEING UPSET BY IT.

REMINDER.

NOTHING IS PERMANENT.

BAD SITUATIONS <u>ALWAYS</u> COME TO AN END.

YOU'LL LOOK BACK AT THAT "BAD MOMENT"

AND REALIZE HOW MUCH IT HELPED YOU

BECOME. THE PERSON YOU ARE TODAY

EMBRACE THE TOUGH TIMES AND

LOOK FOR THE LESSON IN

EVERY CHALLENGE

YOU FACE.

LOOK AT OBSTACLES

AS OPPORTUNITIES TO LEARN AND GROW

CHALLENGES ARE A PART OF LIFE. ACCEPT THEM, AND

APPRECIATE THE MISTAKES THAT PRODUCE WISDOM.

PROBLEMS ARE NOT STOP SIGNS.

THEY ARE OPPORTUNITIES TO DEVELOP

INTO A STRONGER VERSION OF YOURSELF.

START REPLACING,

"WHY IS THIS HAPPENING TO ME?"

WITH

"WHAT IS THIS TRYING TO TEACH ME?"

THERE'S A HIDDEN LESSON TO BE LEARNED

IN EVERY STORM YOU FACE.

STEP OUTSIDE OF YOUR
COMFORT ZONE

DON'T ALLOW THE NEGATIVE THINGS THAT'VE

HAPPENED <u>TO</u> YOU PREVENT YOU FROM THE

POSITIVE THINGS THAT ARE

WAITING <u>FOR</u> YOU.

IT'S NORMAL TO

FEEL NERVOUS ABOUT

STEPPING OUTSIDE OF YOUR

COMFORT ZONE, BUT THE MORE

OPEN YOU ARE TO EXPERIENCING NEW

THINGS, THE MORE CONFIDENT YOU'LL BECOME

IN YOUR ABILITY TO FACE NEW SITUATIONS. PUSHING

YOURSELF TO TRY SOMETHING NEW WILL HELP YOU

<u>GROW AND DEVELOP INTO A STRONGER PERSON</u>.

DIFFICULTIES ARE NECESSARY FOR SUCCESS.

TOUGH TIMES MAY SEEM UNBEARABLE
WHEN YOU'RE GOING THROUGH THEM
BUT THERE IS A PURPOSE FOR YOUR PAIN.

THE CHALLENGES YOU'RE FACING ARE TO PREPARE YOU FOR
SOMETHING BIGGER AND BETTER THAN YOU CAN IMAGINE.
STAY FOCUSED AND KEEP GOING.

SOME OF THE BEST VIEWS COME AFTER THE HARDEST CLIMBS.

ASK FOR HELP

Many of us are silently fighting the exact same battles because we assume we have to deal with difficulties on our own. There are people in your life who have experience overcoming what you're going through. Use others as a resource to overcome the challenges you're facing.

SUCCESS

IS NOT MEASURED BY WHAT YOU AVOID; SUCCESS
IS MEASURED BY WHAT YOU SURVIVE, WHAT YOU
OVERCOME, AND WHAT YOU ACHIEVE,
DESPITE DIFFICULTY.

YOU ARE <u>NOT</u> DEFINED BY YOUR FAILURES. YOU ARE
DEFINED BY YOUR ABILITY TO TAKE ACTION.
EMBRACE EVERY OBSTACLE AND LOOK
FOR THE LESSON IN EVERY LOSS
YOU EXPERIENCE.

BELIEVE IN YOURSELF,

BECAUSE YOU HAVE THE ABILITY TO DEFEAT
ANY STORM THAT COMES INTO YOUR LIFE.

CHAPTER THREE

LUXURY

*YOUR HAPPINESS IS DETERMINED BY YOUR
MINDSET, NOT YOUR CIRCUMSTANCES.
CHOOSING TO BE GRATEFUL IN EVERY
SITUATION IS THE KEY TO CREATING
LUXURY IN YOUR LIFE.*

#GRATITUDE

SOME DAYS, IT FEELS LIKE

EVERYBODY

AROUND YOU IS LIVING

A BETTER LIFE THAN YOU ARE?

This person started a new job.

That person moved into a new house.

This person just bought a new car.

That person got a promotion.

This person just graduated.

This person wrote a book.

That person is getting married.

This person started a business.

That person gets to travel the country.

It's hard to be happy for everyone's
"GREAT ACHIEVEMENTS"
when you compare them to your
"LACK OF ACCOMPLISHMENTS."

Comparing your life to others often makes you question your own:

What's wrong with me?

Why can't I have what others have?

Maybe I'm not good enough...

THE

COMPARISON TRAP

IS SOMETHING WE <u>ALL</u> DEAL WITH

BUT RARELY EVER TALK ABOUT.

WE COMPARE

OUR LIVES ON SOCIAL MEDIA.

WE COMPARE

OUR LOOKS TO CELEBRITIES WE'VE NEVER MET.

WE COMPARE

OUR THINGS, OUR MONEY, OUR APPEARANCE,

OUR EDUCATION, AND OUR CAREERS.

WE EVEN COMPARE OURSELVES TO

WHO WE *THINK* WE SHOULD BE,

AND WHAT WE *WISH* WE HAD.

COMPARING YOURSELF

TO OTHER PEOPLE IS THE

RECIPE FOR

UNHAPPINESS.

IT DESTROYS YOUR CONFIDENCE, ROBS YOU OF

YOUR SELF-ESTEEM, AND CAUSES YOU TO FEEL JEALOUS,

ENVIOUS, ANGRY, INSECURE, AND INFERIOR.

COMPARISONS TRICK YOU INTO

BELIEVING A FASLE REALITY –

THAT EVERYONE ELSE

IS DOING BETTER

THAN YOU ARE.

TO ATTRACT HAPPINESS, ABUNDANCE,

AND PROSPERITY YOU MUST

CELEBRATE

WHO YOU ARE AND

FIND JOY

IN THE QUALITIES THAT MAKE YOU UNIQUE.

YOU MUST REPLACE COMPARISON WITH APPRECIATION,

RECOGNIZE THE POSITIVES IN YOUR LIFE, AND

ACKNOWLEDGE <u>EVERY REASON</u> YOU

HAVE TO BE GRATEFUL.

TO ACHIEVE SUCCESS, *YOU MUST <u>PRACTICE GRATITUDE</u>.*

♛

GRATITUDE

IS YOUR ABILITY TO SEE THE POSITIVE IN EVERYTHING

YOU EXPERIENCE. IT'S BEING THANKFUL FOR THE

THINGS YOU HAVE, ACCEPTING YOURSELF,

AND APPRECIATING YOUR QUALITIES

AND CHARACTERISTICS.

GRATITUDE

IS THE STATE OF BEING AND FEELING GENEROUS.

IT'S THE EMOTION YOU FEEL WHEN YOU GIVE A

COMPLIMENT OR RECEIVE A GIFT. IT'S

ACKNOWLEDGING THE GOOD

THINGS IN YOUR LIFE AND

BEING HAPPY WITH

WHO YOU ARE.

GRATITUDE TURNS *EVERYTHING*

IN YOUR LIFE INTO A

LUXURY,

SIMPLY BY BEING AND FEELING GRATEFUL.

IT'S YOUR UNLIMITED SOURCE OF

HAPPINESS AND THE

KEY TO LIVING

ABUNDANTLY.

WHEN YOU REALIZE THAT

HAPPINESS BEGINS AND ENDS

WITH YOU,

YOU LOSE THE DESIRE TO

COMPETE WITH EVERYONE ELSE.

BY APPRECIATING WHAT YOU HAVE, YOUR CONFIDENCE

WILL INCREASE. YOU'LL BECOME MORE OPTIMISTIC

AND POSITIVE, AND YOU'LL STOP CARING

ABOUT HOW YOU RANK IN

COMPARISON TO

OTHER PEOPLE.

YOU DECIDE.

NO MATTER HOW LITTLE YOU **THINK** YOU HAVE THERE IS SOMEONE RIGHT NOW WHO IS WISHING FOR A LIFE LIKE YOURS, AND PRAYING FOR THE THINGS YOU TAKE FOR GRANTED. DON'T COMPARE YOUR LIFE TO WHAT YOU **THINK** IT SHOULD BE, TREAT IT AS THE <u>LUXURY</u> THAT IT'S MEANT TO BE.

—

USE THE FOLLOWING SIMPLE ACTIONS TO PRACTICE **GRATITUDE:**

START AN
ABUNDANCE JOURNAL

An abundance journal is a way to reflect on the positive experiences that happened to you during the week. Writing or typing your positive experiences reminds you of the phenomenal things in your life, the amazing qualities you possess, and all of the reasons you have to be grateful.

Once a week, on your phone or on paper, record five things you're grateful for in your life. These can be people, events, experiences, characteristics, or anything you appreciate. Reflect on how your life would be without these things.

The goal of abundance journaling is to remind yourself of everything you have to be grateful for in your life, and to enjoy the positive emotions that come with reflecting on them.

CARRY A GRATITUDE ROCK

Sometimes, we may take things in our lives for granted because we've gotten so used to having them. A gratitude rock is a way to remind yourself to always be grateful, and to always show appreciation for what you have.

A gratitude rock allows you to experience immediate feelings of happiness, appreciation, and satisfaction. If you happen to feel upset, defeated, or stressed out, using a gratitude rock can help shift your mood from negative to positive within seconds.

Find a rock or stone that is small enough to fit in your pocket and carry it with you at all times. Any time you reach in your pocket to grab your phone or your keys, your gratitude rock will be there. Whenever you touch your gratitude rock, think of something you're grateful for. You may be grateful for your job, your home, your friends, or your family. There are no restrictions to what you can choose. Using a gratitude rock will get you in the habit of practicing gratitude without having to think about it.

A grateful heart is a magnet for happiness.

Always find a reason to practice gratitude.

ALWAYS FIND GRATITUDE

FIND GRATITUDE FOR THE FRESH START YOU'RE GIVEN EVERY DAY.

FIND GRATITUDE FOR CHALLENGES THAT ALLOW YOU TO GROW.

FIND GRATITUDE FOR THE PEOPLE IN YOUR LIFE WHO LOVE YOU.

FIND GRATITUDE FOR THE OPPORTUNITIES YOU'VE BEEN GIVEN.

FIND GRATITUDE FOR RELATIONSHIPS THAT DIDN'T WORK OUT.

FIND GRATITUDE FOR THE PEACEFUL MOMENTS IN YOUR DAY.

FIND GRATITUDE FOR THE 2ND CHANCES YOU'VE BEEN GIVEN.

FIND GRATITUDE FOR HAVING A PLACE TO SLEEP AT NIGHT.

FIND GRATITUDE FOR YOUR ACCOMPLISHMENTS SO FAR.

FIND GRATITUDE FOR THE VACATIONS YOU GET TO TAKE.

FIND GRATITUDE FOR THE CLOTHES YOU'RE WEARING.

FIND GRATITUDE FOR THE LESSONS YOU'VE LEARNED.

FIND GRATITUDE FOR THE PEOPLE WHO INSPIRE YOU.

FIND GRATITUDE FOR COMPLIMENTS YOU RECEIVE.

FIND GRATITUDE WHEN YOU FEEL OVERWHELMED.

FIND GRATITUDE FOR WAKING UP THIS MORNING.

FIND GRATITUDE FOR THE FOOD YOU HAVE.

FIND GRATITUDE FOR NEW RELATIONSHIPS.

FIND GRATITUDE FOR THE ABILITY TO READ.

FIND GRATITUDE FOR ELECTRICITY.

FIND GRATITUDE FOR KINDNESS.

FIND GRATITUDE FOR YOUR JOB.

FIND GRATITUDE FOR HUMOR.

A "LACK OF MENTALITY"
CREATES A "LESS THAN" REALITY

WHAT YOU HAVE

CAN TURN INTO

WHAT YOU HAD

IN A MATTER OF SECONDS.

APPRECIATE EVERY SINGLE MOMENT YOU HAVE
BEFORE IT BECOME A MEMORY.

MAKE A VICTORY JAR

A victory jar is a way to celebrate your accomplishments and positive experiences. It's a reminder for you to take time and appreciate the wins in your life, big or small. Victories are experiences that make you feel positive and appreciative. A victory may be accomplishing a goal, receiving a compliment, or simply eating your favorite meal. **Follow the steps below to make your victory jar.**

1.   Find an empty jar, cup, or container.
2.   On a small piece of paper, write down a recent positive experience that happened to you, and the date it occurred.
3.   Put your piece of paper in your victory jar, and place your jar in an area where you will see it often.
4.   Continue adding victories to your jar as soon as they happen.
5.   When you need a dose of motivation or encouragement open your jar and reflect on the victories of your past.

Victory jars use the wins in your life to motivate you and help you feel more accomplished, happy, and optimistic.

SEND GRATITUDE TEXTS

Showing gratitude to others is a way to display your appreciation for the people in your life who've made a positive impact. A gratitude text can help you do this. Gratitude texts create strong positive emotions within you and for the person receiving the text. **Use the steps below to begin sending out gratitude texts.**

1. Think about someone who made a positive impact in your life. This could be a relative, friend, teacher, or colleague.
2. Reflect on the qualities of this person and the moments that made a difference for you.
3. Type your text. Describe specifically what this person did, why you're grateful for this person, and how this person's behavior has affected your life positively.
4. Send your text. If you are able to meet the person face-to-face, read the text aloud to them.

Gratitude Text Example:

"Hi _____ (insert the person's name),

I want to tell you that I appreciate you and the positive impact you make in my life. Thank you for _____ (insert the reason why you're grateful for them). I would not be the person I am today without you. I want you to know that I'm grateful for our relationship."

Thanking someone is a powerful way to experience the greatest benefits of gratitude.

TAKE A 30-DAY BREAK
FROM SOCIAL MEDIA

Social media connects us to the world. It's a great way to stay in contact with friends, family members, and peers. Social media can also be dangerous because many of us spend hours each day scrolling through our timelines, looking at life updates from other people, and comparing our lives to their lives.

We often see the best version of someone else and compare it to the worst qualities within ourself, destroying our self-esteem.

Taking a 30-day break from social media is a way to eliminate distractions from the lives of other people to focus on YOU. **Follow the steps below to get started.**

1. Delete all social media apps from your phone. You can download the apps again in 30 days, and all of your information will still be there waiting for you.
2. Log out of all social media accounts on your laptop, desktops, tablets, and other mobile devices.
3. Replace the time you were spending on social media with something productive and more meaningful to you.

By taking a break from social media, you'll do less comparing, have more time in your day to be productive, and gain a better sense of focus.

THE BRIDGE TO YOUR ABUNDANCE STARTS WITH GRATITUDE.

EMBRACE THE PACE OF YOUR OWN JOURNEY.

APPRECIATE YOUR PROGRESS, AND

REJECT PERFECTIONISM.

DON'T LET THE LIVES OF OTHER PEOPLE

MAKE YOU FEEL LIKE YOUR LIFE

IS NOT ENOUGH.

FIND INSPIRATION WITHOUT COMPARISON.

CELEBRATE YOUR WINS, ACKNOWLEDGE

YOUR VICTORIES, AND

BELIEVE IN YOURSELF,

BECAUSE YOU HAVE EVERYTHING YOU

NEED TO CREATE TRUE HAPPINESS.

CHAPTER FOUR

LIMITLESS

*ANYTHING YOU WANT TO ACCOMPLISH CAN
BE ACHIEVED. THERE ARE NO LIMITS TO
WHAT YOU CAN DO. THE SECRET TO SUCCESS
IS FOUND IN YOUR DAILY ROUTINE.*

#SUCCESSHABITS

IF YOU COULD HAVE GUARANTEED

SUCCESS

IN ANYTHING YOU CHOOSE

WHAT WOULD YOU BE DOING?

_____

WHAT CAREER WOULD YOU HAVE?

WHAT IDEA WOULD YOU PURSUE?

WHAT BUSINESS WOULD YOU START?

WHAT BOOK WOULD YOU WRITE?

WHAT DREAM WOULD YOU LIVE?

WHO WOULD YOU HAVE IN YOUR LIFE?

MANY OF US HAVE

HIGH ASPIRATIONS

AND

GREAT EXPECTATIONS

FOR OUR LIVES.

WE *PLAN* TO ACHIEVE EXCITING THINGS BUT WE

SELL OURSELVES SHORT

BY NOT TAKING PROPER ACTION.

EVERY MOTIVATIONAL SPEAKER,
SELF-HELP BOOK, AND "EXPERT" TELLS US,

"THE MOST EFFECTIVE WAY TO SHAPE YOUR FUTURE IS TO SET INTENTIONAL GOALS."

YES, YOUR GOALS ARE IMPORTANT. THEY ARE THE ROAD
MAPS THAT GUIDE YOU ON YOUR SUCCESS JOURNEY.
SETTING GOALS GIVES YOU PURPOSE AND
DIRECTION – SHOWING YOU WHAT
IS POSSIBLE FOR YOUR LIFE.

BUT,

MOST OF US HAVE
BEEN SETTING GOALS FOR YEARS.
WE HAVE EVERY INTENTION TO ACCOMPLISH
OUR GOALS, BUT WE GET DISTRACTED, LOSE FOCUS,
LOSE MOMENTUM, AND QUIT BEFORE ACHIEVING THEM.

We never discover how great we truly are because we keep getting sidetracked by secondary activity.

WHAT'S STOPPING YOU

FROM ACCOMPLISHING YOUR GOALS?

IS IT PROCRASTINATION?

FEAR? LAZINESS MAYBE?

EXCUSES? GIVING UP AFTER

ONE TRY? SPENDING TOO

MUCH TIME ON SOCIAL

MEDIA? ARE YOU PUTTING

OTHER PEOPLE'S PRIORITIES BEFORE

YOUR OWN? ARE YOU AFRAID TO STEP OUTSIDE

OF YOUR COMFORT ZONE? ARE

UNPRODUCTIVE ACTIVITIES

SLOWING YOU

DOWN?

IN ORDER TO REACH

THE LEVEL OF GREATNESS

YOU DESIRE, YES, IT'S IMPORTANT TO *SET*

GOALS, BUT IT'S NOT ENOUGH TO

ACHIEVE SUCCESS.

THERE'S A GAP BETWEEN
WHERE YOU CURRENTLY ARE
AND WHERE YOU WANT TO BE.
IN ORDER TO TURN YOUR DREAMS
INTO A REALITY, IT'S NECESSARY
FOR YOU TO FILL THAT GAP WITH

DAILY ACTION.

IN ORDER TO ACHIEVE SUCCESS,
YOU MUST FORM SUCCESS HABITS.

♛

HABITS

ARE THE ACTIONS YOU PERFORM REPEATEDLY
AND THE DECISIONS YOU MAKE REGULARLY.

THEY'RE THE BEHAVIORS IN YOUR LIFE THAT HAPPEN SO
OFTEN, THEY BECOME A PART OF WHO YOU ARE.

HABITS CAN HAVE A
NEGATIVE IMPACT ON YOUR LIFE,
OR BE INSTRUMENTAL TO YOUR SUCCESS.
YOU MUST MAKE THE CHOICE TO FORM HABITS
THAT DRIVE YOU CLOSER TO THE LIFE YOU DESIRE.

GOALS SET DIRECTION,
ACTION CREATES PROGRESS,
BUT YOUR **HABITS** DECIDE YOUR FUTURE.

Never limit the

VISION

you have for yourself

based on where you are

right now.

WHERE DO YOU WANT TO BE
IN THE NEXT 5 YEARS?

WHAT DO YOU NEED TO DO?

WHAT GOALS DO YOU NEED TO SET?

WHAT RESOURCES DO YOU NEED?

WHAT CHANGE NEEDS TO TAKE PLACE?

WHAT SKILLS ARE REQUIRED?

WHAT TYPE OF PERSON DO YOU NEED TO BECOME?

DO SOMETHING TODAY THAT YOUR FUTURE SELF WILL THANK YOU FOR. USE THESE SIMPLE ACTIONS TO BUILD SUCCESS HABITS:

Visualize Your Goals

WRITE DOWN YOUR BIGGEST LIFE GOALS. THEN, TAKE A MOMENT TO IMAGINE HOW YOU WOULD FEEL IF EVERY ONE OF YOUR GOALS WAS ACHIEVED. THINK ABOUT THE EMOTIONS YOU WOULD EXPERIENCE IF YOUR VISION BECAME YOUR NEW REALITY. VISUALIZE THE KIND OF LIFE YOU WANT AND YOUR REALITY WILL START TO MATCH YOUR VISION.

IDENTIFY ONE GOAL EACH DAY
AND WRITE IT DOWN ON A WHITEBOARD

Writing down your daily goals is a way to narrow your focus and increase your productivity. Using a whiteboard to write down your goals trains your brain to focus on making progress every day, and prevents you from overloading your day with time-wasters and unneeded tasks.

Every morning, on a small whiteboard (which can be purchased at your local dollar store), write down one goal you want to accomplish for the day. Your one goal can be:

- A small task you've been putting off completing for awhile, such as doing laundry.
- A small action you can take toward a larger goal, such as applying for one job or spending one hour to work on your side hustle.
- Your #1 priority for the day.

Focus on one goal and one goal only. By doing this, you'll find it easier to prioritize the important things in your day while eliminating activities that have nothing to do with your success journey. Setting daily goals will change your life for the better. It will drive you closer to your dreams and help you establish productive habits.

MAKE A "TO-DON'T" LIST

WE ALL HAVE DISTRACTIONS IN OUR LIVES THAT PREVENT US FROM OUR DAILY GOALS AND PRIORITIES. A "TO-DON'T" LIST IS A LIST OF TASKS THAT EAT UP YOUR TIME AND PROVIDE LITTLE TO NO REWARD FOR COMPLETING THEM. SPENDING HOURS ON SOCIAL MEDIA, BINGE-WATCHING SHOWS, AND PLAYING VIDEO GAMES ARE ALL EXAMPLES OF ACTIVITIES THAT CAN BE ADDED TO YOUR LIST. ONCE YOU KNOW WHAT YOUR DISTRACTIONS ARE, YOU CAN BEGIN BUILDING A DEFENSE AGAINST THEM.

BREAK YOUR LONG-TERM GOALS

INTO SMALL DAILY ACTIONS

5-YEAR GOAL

What is a big goal you want to accomplish

within the next five years?

↓

1-YEAR GOAL

What is one action you can take <u>this year</u> toward your goal?

↓

MONTHLY GOAL

What is one action you can take <u>this month</u> toward your goal?

↓

WEEKLY GOAL

What is one action you can take <u>this week</u> toward your goal?

↓

DAILY GOAL

What is one action you can take <u>today</u> toward your goal?

↓

RIGHT NOW

What is one action you can take <u>right now</u> toward your goal?

ESTABLISH A DAILY ROUTINE

A ROUTINE IS A SET OF ACTIONS AND HABITS YOU PERFORM ON A REGULAR BASIS TO HELP YOU STAY ORGANIZED. ROUTINES PROVIDE STRUCTURE TO YOUR DAY AND ALLOW YOU TO CONTROL WHAT YOU GET DONE. HAVING A ROUTINE HELPS YOU REMOVE DISTRACTIONS FROM YOUR LIFE, AND HELPS YOU MAKE CONSISTENT PROGRESS TOWARD YOUR GOALS. HERE ARE SOME HABITS YOU CAN ADD TO YOUR ROUTINE:

JOURNAL	MEDITATE
CREATE A TO-DO LIST	SCHEDULE YOUR DAY
RESPOND TO MESSAGES	IDENTIFY YOUR TOP PRIORITY
EAT A HEALTHY SNACK	LEARN SOMETHING NEW
SPEND TIME WITH LOVED ONES	LISTEN TO MUSIC
EXERCISE/STRETCH	MAKE YOUR BED
READ SOMETHING INFORMATIVE	PRACTICE SELF-CARE
WATCH SOMETHING INFORMATIVE	REVIEW YOUR GOALS
PRACTICE GRATITUDE	WORK ON A SIDE HUSTLE
SET TIME LIMITS FOR CERTAIN ACTIVITIES	PREPARE FOR THE NEXT DAY
REFLECT ON YOUR ACCOMPLISHMENTS	MAKE ONE BUSINESS CONNECTION

GET AN ACCOUNTABILITY PARTNER

You're more likely to take action when someone else is helping you keep track of your progress. An accountability partner is a person who helps you identify your goals, and monitors the progress you make until you achieve each goal. Having an accountability partner is like having an unlimited source of encouragement and feedback. The role of an accountability partner is to act as your coach or guide, motivating you to take action when you need an extra push.

- Choose someone you trust to be your accountability partner.
- Talk to your accountability partner about your dreams and aspirations.
- Work with your accountability partner to set long-term goals.
- Discuss what daily actions you can take to reach your long-term goals.
- Schedule regular check-ins with your accountability partner over the phone, through text, or in-person to evaluate and discuss the progress toward your goals.

DEVELOP MILESTONES TOWARD YOUR GOALS

Sometimes, it's hard to stay focused on your goal because it seems so far away from completion. Create milestones that will help you move toward your goals without losing focus. For example, if you're looking for a new job, commit to applying for one job each week until you find the opportunity you're looking for. It's easier to stay focused on milestones because they seem more reasonable, yet, they still send you in the same direction.

REWARD YOURSELF

FOR MAKING PROGRESS

A REWARD SYSTEM IS A WAY TO ENCOURAGE YOURSELF TO MAKE PROGRESS TOWARD YOUR GOALS. WHEN YOU FINISH A TASK, REWARD YOURSELF WITH SOMETHING YOU ENJOY, LIKE GOING TO THE MOVIES, GOING OUT TO EAT, PURCHASING A SMALL GIFT FOR YOURSELF, OR TAKING PERSONAL TIME TO RELAX. LEARN TO CELEBRATE YOUR PROGRESS, NOT JUST THE FINAL DESTINATION. ANY SMALL STEP TOWARD ACHIEVING YOUR GOALS IS WORTH ACKNOWLEDGING.

WHAT NEEDS TO HAPPEN FOR YOU TO SAY,

"THIS HAS BEEN THE MOST AMAZING YEAR OF MY LIFE?"

WHAT CHANGES DO YOU NEED TO MAKE? WHAT
ACTION DO YOU NEED TO TAKE? WHAT TYPE
OF PERSON DO YOU NEED TO BECOME TO
ACHIEVE YOUR MOST DESIRED GOALS?
WHAT WILL YOU DO TODAY THAT
WILL BE WORTH TALKING
ABOUT ONE YEAR
FROM NOW?

ENVISION WHAT YOU WANT TO ACCOMPLISH. WRITE
OUT YOUR GOALS AND SET A DEADLINE BY WHICH YOU
WANT TO ACHIEVE THEM. ANTICIPATE THINGS GOING
WRONG ALONG THE WAY SO YOU HAVE A PLAN TO
ADDRESS CHALLENGES. LEARN TO SAY "NO" TO THINGS
THAT HAVE <u>NOTHING</u> TO DO WITH YOUR FUTURE.

BELIEVE IN YOURSELF

AND THE LIMITATIONS IN LIFE WILL DISAPPEAR.

CHAPTER FIVE

POWER

SUCCESS CANNOT BE ACHIEVED ALONE. THE KEY TO ACCESSING GREATER OPPORTUNITIES IS TO BUILD POWERFUL RELATIONSHIPS.

#POWERCIRCLE

"MY FRIENDS DETERMINE THE LEVEL OF MY SUCCESS."

THAT'S NOT A STATEMENT MANY OF US ARE
WILLING TO AGREE WITH OR ACCEPT.

MOST PEOPLE DON'T REALIZE

RELATIONSHIPS

DICTATE YOUR OPPORTUNITIES,

SHAPE YOUR PERSONALITY,

AND DECIDE THE DIRECTION

OF YOUR FUTURE.

THE FIVE PEOPLE

YOU SPEND THE MOST

TIME WITH MAKE UP YOUR

INNER CIRCLE,

AND WHETHER YOU LIKE IT OR NOT, MANY

OF YOUR THOUGHTS, BELIEFS,

BEHAVIORS, AND HABITS

ARE INFLUENCED BY

THESE FIVE PEOPLE.

———————

THE MISTAKE WE MAKE IS

ALLOWING PEOPLE INTO OUR CIRCLE

WHO DON'T DESERVE A

FRONT ROW SEAT IN OUR LIFE.

MANY OF US HAVE A HARD TIME RECOGNIZING OUR

TOXIC RELATIONSHIPS.

WE LET PEOPLE WHO ADD NO VALUE TO

OUR LIVES INFLUENCE OUR WAY OF THINKING.

WE QUESTION

WHY WE CAN'T ACCOMPLISH OUR GOALS,

BUT FAIL TO QUESTION

WHY WE KEEP CERTAIN PEOPLE IN OUR CIRCLE.

JUST BECAUSE THEY'RE IN YOUR CIRCLE

DOESN'T MEAN THEY'RE

IN YOUR CORNER.

SOME OF YOUR CLOSEST

FRIENDS AND FAMILY MEMBERS

MAY BE THE ONES SECRETELY COMPETING WITH YOU.

THEY LOVE WHAT YOU'RE DOING,

BUT HATE THAT YOU'RE THE ONE DOING IT

INSTEAD OF THEM.

———————————

SOME OF US

HOLD ON TO RELATIONSHIPS

THAT EXPIRED <u>YEARS</u> AGO.

WE STAY LOYAL TO CERTAIN PEOPLE,

BUT THOSE *SAME* PEOPLE MAY BE THE ONES

PREVENTING US FROM PURSUING OUR PASSION,

DISTRACTING US FROM WORKING ON OUR GOALS,

AND DISCOURAGING US FROM ACHIEVING OUR DREAM.

JUST BECAUSE YOU HAVE

HISTORY

WITH A PERSON DOESN'T MEAN YOU HAVE A

FUTURE TOGETHER.

EVERY RELATIONSHIP
HAS A PURPOSE.

SOME PEOPLE

WERE MEANT TO BE IN YOUR LIFE

FOR A REASON, OTHERS FOR A SEASON.

IT'S UP TO YOU TO MAKE SURE YOUR RELATIONSHIPS

MATCH THE LEVEL OF SUCCESS YOU WANT TO ACHIEVE.

IN ORDER TO CREATE

POWERFUL OPPORTUNITIES

YOU MUST CONNECT WITH PEOPLE WHO ARE ON A
MISSION TO ACHIEVE GREATNESS.

————————

YOU MUST BE PICKY WITH WHO YOU SPEND YOUR
TIME WITH, AND WHO YOU ALLOW TO
INFLUENCE YOUR FUTURE.

————————

YOU MUST REMOVE TOXIC RELATIONSHIPS AND
SURROUND YOURSELF WITH PEOPLE WHO
HAVE AN EXTREME LEVEL OF
DETERMINATION TO
REACH THEIR
GOALS.

————————

TO ACHIEVE SUCCESS,
YOU MUST DEVELOP A POWER CIRCLE.

♛

YOUR

POWER CIRCLE

IS THE GROUP OF PEOPLE IN YOUR LIFE

WHO ARE DEDICATED TO EACH OTHER'S

SUCCESS, AND SHARE SIMILAR GOALS,

DREAMS AND ASPIRATIONS.

THEY'RE PEOPLE WHO ARE POSITIVE, UPLIFTING, AND

OPTIMISTIC. THEY ENCOURAGE YOU TO LIVE YOUR

DREAM, MOTIVATE YOU TO TAKE ACTION,

AND HOLD YOU ACCOUNTABLE

FOR REACHING SUCCESS.

HAVING A POWER CIRCLE DOES NOT REQUIRE YOU TO CUT

OFF YOUR PREVIOUS RELATIONSHIPS, IT JUST MEANS

YOU ARE BEING SELECTIVE ABOUT WHO YOU SHARE

YOUR VISION WITH, AND WHO YOU LOOK TO FOR

INSPIRATION.

ARE THE PEOPLE IN YOUR CURRENT CIRCLE LIMITING YOUR VISION OR HELPING YOU TURN IT INTO A REALITY? ARE THEY INSPIRING YOU TO BECOME THE GREATEST VERSION OF YOURSELF OR REMINDING YOU WHERE YOU FALL SHORT? WHO ARE YOU ALLOWING TO INFLUENCE YOUR SUCCESS?

———

USE THE FOLLOWING SIMPLE ACTIONS TO ESTABLISH A **POWER CIRCLE:**

EVALUATE YOUR RELATIONSHIPS

WHO ARE THE FIVE PEOPLE YOU SPEND TIME WITH THE MOST?

- Do you share similar interests?
- Do they hold you accountable and push you to accomplish your goals?
- Do they elevate you or bring you down?
- Do they admire your qualities or criticize them?
- Are they motivators or energy drainers?
- Are they bringing happiness to your life or adding drama to it?
- Are they adding value to your relationship or bringing stress to it?

Evaluating your relationships will help you determine who to keep in your power circle, and who to keep at a distance.

RECOGNIZE COMPETITION
DISGUISED AS SUPPORT

SOME OF THE PEOPLE WHO ARE CLOSE _TO_ YOU

DON'T NECESSARILY WANT THE BEST _FOR_ YOU.

THEY PRETEND THEY'RE HAPPY FOR YOU BUT ARE

SECRETELY ENVIOUS OF YOUR ELEVATION.

THEY AREN'T COMFORTABLE WITH

YOUR EVOLUTION BECAUSE

THEY HAVEN'T EVOLVED.

PAY ATTENTION TO THE

PATTERNS

IN A PERSON'S BEHAVIOR SO YOU

CAN IDENTIFY WHO IS SUPPORTING YOU AND

WHO IS COMPETING AGAINST YOU.

No matter how good your outfit looks, how much positivity you post, or how creative your captions are, some people will never hit the "like" button because it's **YOU**.

Jealousy can make your "friends" scroll right past your progress.

ELIMINATE NEGATIVE RELATIONSHIPS

SOME PEOPLE TRY TO DO EVERYTHING IN THEIR
POWER TO BREAK YOUR SPIRIT.

YOU TELL THEM YOUR DREAM,
THEY TELL YOU WHY IT WON'T WORK.
YOU MAKE PROGRESS TOWARD YOUR GOALS,
THEY REMIND YOU THAT YOU STILL HAVE A
LONG WAY TO GO.

**STOP HOLDING ONTO
EXPIRED RELATIONSHIPS.**

YOUR "DAY ONES" MAY BE PREVENTING YOU FROM
REACHING THE LEVEL OF SUCCESS YOU DESIRE.
REPLACE NEGATIVE RELATIONSHIPS WITH PEOPLE
WHO INSPIRE YOU TO TAKE ACTION, AND PEOPLE
WHO FORCE YOU TO LEVEL UP.

SOMEONE ELSE'S OPINION OF YOU IS A REFLECTION OF WHO THEY ARE, NOT WHO YOU ARE.

THEIR WORDS AND ACTIONS REPRESENT THEIR LIFE, <u>NOT</u> YOURS. OUTSIDE PERSPECTIVES DO NOT DEFINE YOUR REALITY.

MEET NEW PEOPLE AND BUILD NEW RELATIONSHIPS

BUILD RELATIONSHIPS WITH PEOPLE WHO ENCOURAGE YOU TO LEARN, GROW, AND DEVELOP INTO THE BEST VERSION OF YOURSELF.

- Attend a social event that appeals to your interests, or host your own event.
- Invite a neighbor or co-worker out for dinner and accept invitations from others.
- Reach out to like-minded people on social media.
- Start a conversation with a former classmate.
- Join social groups for meeting new people.
- Join a gym or an intramural sports team.
- Take time to unplug from your mobile device and start a conversation with someone around you.

FIND A MENTOR.

FIND SOMEONE WHO IS SUCCESSFULLY DOING

WHAT YOU WANT TO DO AND BUILD A

RELATIONSHIP WITH THAT PERSON.

CALL THEM, TAKE THEM OUT TO

LUNCH, AND FIND OUT WHAT

THEY DID TO REACH THEIR

LEVEL OF SUCCESS. THEN

FOLLOW THE SAME

STRATEGIES THEY

USED TO BECOME

SUCCESSFUL.

NOT EVERYONE DESERVES TO BE AROUND YOU.
LET GO OF THE PEOPLE IN YOUR LIFE WHO
AREN'T ADDING VALUE, AND CONNECT
WITH PEOPLE WHO ARE ON
A MISSION TO

REINVENT THEMSELVES.

BECOME FRIENDS WITH PEOPLE WHO WILL
CELEBRATE YOUR SUCCESS AS IF IT WERE THEIR OWN.

BUILD RELATIONSHIPS

WITH PEOPLE WHO WILL
HELP YOU MINIMIZE YOUR MISTAKES
AND MAXIMIZE YOUR OPPORTUNITIES.

DEVELOP A POWER CIRCLE THAT WILL INCREASE
YOUR NET WORTH, PUT YOU CLOSER TO YOUR
DREAMS, AND INSPIRE YOU TO ALWAYS

BELIEVE IN YOURSELF.

CHAPTER SIX

MA$TERMIND

*YOUR SUCCESS WILL LEAD TO MORE MONEY
AND THE OPPORTUNITY TO BECOME
WEALTHY. THE KEY TO BUILDING WEALTH IS
MAKING SMART DECISIONS WITH YOUR
MONEY SO IT GROWS OVER TIME.*

#FINANCIALLITERACY

WE LIVE IN A WORLD WHERE

BEING BROKE

AND FEELING UNHAPPY IS MORE COMMON THAN

BUILDING WEALTH

AND LIVING ABUNDANTLY.

SOME OF US HAVE GOTTEN SO USE TO LIVING

PAYCHECK TO PAYCHECK

THAT IT'S BECOME THE NORM.

WE GET SO BUSY PAYING OFF DEBT,

WE BARELY HAVE MONEY TO

INVEST IN OUR FUTURE.

AND MANY OF US HAVEN'T BECOME

WEALTHY SIMPLY BECAUSE

WE DON'T *BELIEVE* IT'S POSSIBLE.

MOST OF US WEREN'T TAUGHT ABOUT FINANCES GROWING UP,

AND BECAUSE WE'VE HAD VERY LITTLE CONVERSATIONS ABOUT MONEY, WE'VE MADE MANY MISTAKES WHEN IT COMES TO MANAGING IT.

_____

SOME OF US HAVE HAD SO MANY

FINANCIAL SETBACKS

THAT WE'VE DEVELOPED A

SCARCITY MENTALITY

– WE FOCUS ON WHAT WE CAN'T AFFORD, WE DON'T THINK WE'RE WORTHY OF MAKING A LOT OF MONEY, AND WE BELIEVE THAT BECOMING WEALTHY IS TOO GOOD TO BE TRUE.

STOP ALLOWING YOUR CURRENT

FINANCIAL SITUATION,

TO DESTROY YOUR

WEALTH ASPIRATIONS.

NO MATTER

HOW MUCH DEBT YOU'RE IN,

NO MATTER

WHAT MISTAKES YOU'VE MADE IN THE PAST,

NO MATTER

HOW MUCH MONEY YOU HAVE, OR DON'T HAVE,

YOU CAN ACHIEVE FINANCIAL FREEDOM BY FIRST

CHANGING THE WAY YOU INTERACT WITH MONEY.

MOST PEOPLE MAKE THE MISTAKE OF BELIEVING

WEALTH IS *ONLY* AVAILABLE

TO THOSE WHO ALREADY HAVE MONEY.

SOME PEOPLE EVEN FEEL UNCOMFORTABLE

ADMITTING THEY WANT TO MAKE A LOT OF MONEY.

MONEY IS SIMPLY A RESOURCE THAT ALLOWS YOU TO

LIVE COMFORTABLY. IT PROVIDES YOU WITH

SECURITY, STABILITY, AND FREEDOM. IT

HELPS YOU TO ESTABLISH A BETTER

LIFE FOR YOURSELF AND THE

PEOPLE AROUND YOU.

BUILDING WEALTH IS A RESULT OF

SMART DECISIONS

YOU MAKE WITH YOUR MONEY,

NOT THE AMOUNT OF MONEY YOU MAKE.

THE ONLY THING STANDING BETWEEN YOU AND LIVING A LIFE OF

FINANCIAL FREEDOM

IS THE ACTION YOU TAKE TO MAKE IT A REALITY.

_____

YOU MUST

SHIFT YOUR MENTALITY

FROM THINKING THAT YOU AREN'T WORTHY OF MAKING
A LOT OF MONEY TO BELIEVING THAT YOU CAN,
AND YOU WILL BECOME WEALTHY.

YOU MUST SET FINANCIAL GOALS, UNDERSTAND HOW
TO MANAGE YOUR FINANCES, AND REMOVE ANY TOXIC
MONEY HABITS KEEPING YOU IN DEBT.

YOU MUST INVEST YOUR MONEY SO IT CAN
GROW INTO GENERATIONAL WEALTH
FOR YOU AND YOUR FAMILY.

TO ACHIEVE SUCCESS,
YOU MUST INCREASE YOUR FINANCIAL LITERACY.

FINANCIAL LITERACY

IS THE UNDERSTANDING OF TOPICS THAT
INVOLVE MONEY, INCLUDING PERSONAL
FINANCE, INVESTING, AND BUILDING WEALTH.

IT'S LEARNING HOW TO MANAGE YOUR MONEY
EFFECTIVELY, AND UNDERSTANDING HOW TO
REMOVE TOXIC MONEY HABITS, HOW TO
MAKE SMART MONEY DECISIONS, AND
HOW TO GET RID OF DEBT AND
INVEST FOR YOUR FUTURE.

FINANCIAL LITERACY
IS THE FOUNDATION FOR CREATING
GENERATIONAL WEALTH AND THE PATHWAY
TO FINANCIAL INDEPENDENCE.

WHAT SEPARATES THE PEOPLE WHO
BECOME WEALTHY AND THE PEOPLE
WHO JUST DREAM ABOUT IT?

**BELIEVING IT'S POSSIBLE TO BUILD
WEALTH, AND COMMITTING TO MAKING
IT HAPPEN, ONE STEP AT A TIME.**

WHAT ACTION WILL YOU TAKE TODAY
TO ESTABLISH WEALTH AND FINANCIAL
FREEDOM FOR YOUR FUTURE?

———

USE THE FOLLOWING SIMPLE
ACTIONS TO
BUILD WEALTH:

CREATE A BUDGET TO TAKE CONTROL OF YOUR SPENDING

In order to manage your money, you have to know how much is coming in, and how much is going out. Having a budget gives you 100% control of your money by allowing you to estimate your income and expenses over time.

Having a budget helps you understand your relationship with money and allows you to identify your spending habits. A common rule to successful budgeting is to always spend less than what you earn. This will have you save money, stay out of debt, and allow you to invest for your future.

Download the Mint app to budget and track your spending.

Mint allows you to manage all of your finances from one place. With Mint, you can easily create budgets, categorize expenses, set up reminders of when bills are due, and monitor your credit.

AUTOMATE YOUR SAVINGS

One of the hardest parts about saving money every month is remembering to transfer the funds. Automating your savings means you're putting money to the side every month without having to think about it.

To get started, set up a reoccurring transfer from your checking account to your savings account, or have a portion of your paycheck go directly into a savings account each time you get paid.

Automating your savings eliminates the temptation to spend money, and it helps you stay consistent with your savings goals.

START AN EMERGENCY FUND TO COVER UNEXPECTED EVENTS

An emergency fund is a stash of money set aside to cover unplanned events like job loss, medical expenses, or emergency car repairs. Having an emergency fund will help keep your stress level down because it allows you to prepare for financial emergencies that are out of your control.

Your emergency fund should have money to cover your expenses for three to six months. How much you have in your fund depends on the amount of money you spend each month.

To begin saving for your emergency fund, start by putting $25 away each month until you reach $250. Then increase the amount you save each month to $50 until your emergency fund has enough savings to cover expenses for three to six months. It may take some time, but soon you'll have your emergency fund completely filled with money to cover unexpected expenses.

START A RAINY DAY FUND
TO COVER OUT-OF-BUDGET EXPENSES

A rainy day fund is a stash of money set aside to cover one-time expenses that fall outside of your normal budget. Rainy day funds are used to pay for things like broken appliances, minor car expenses, and unexpected bills.

Rainy day funds help you cover unexpected expenses without having to borrow money and go into debt. It also prevents you from having to use money from your main checking account to unexpected expenses. Your rainy day fund should be between $250 and $500 to cover out-of-budget expenses.

To begin saving for your rainy day fund, start by putting $25 away each month until you reach $250. Then work toward reaching $500. When unplanned expenses occur, you'll be at ease knowing you have funds to cover them.

ELIMINATE DEBT TO BECOME FINANCIALLY INDEPENDENT

Anything owed to someone else is considered debt. It's common to owe money on credit card bills, student loans, and other debts but it's important to take action to eliminate your debts as soon as possible. Debt is the enemy of wealth. It causes stress, anger, fear, anxiety, and depression. Debt destroys your credit score, takes away from your happiness, and robs you of your freedom. To establish wealth, you must first take the proper action to eliminate as much debt as you possibly can. By choosing to pay off your debts, you will have more money in the future.

Use the Snowball Method to get out of debt.

The Snowball Method is a commonly used strategy for getting out of debt. You simply pay your smallest debts off first. Then, once the small debts are paid off, you take the money you were using to pay off the small debts, and pay toward your larger debts until those are paid off as well.

To use the Snowball Method for eliminating debt:

1. List all of your debts from smallest to largest.
2. Make minimum payments toward your smallest debt until it is paid off.
3. Use any extra money you have to make additional payments toward your smallest debt.
4. When your smallest debt is gone, start making minimum payments toward your next debt until that one is paid off.

Repeat these steps until all of your debt is paid in full.

The Snowball Method is designed to help you change your behavior with money so you never go into overwhelming debt again. By doing this, you'll gain a sense of accomplishment and relief when you begin to see your debts disappear.

UNDERSTAND YOUR
CREDIT SCORE

Your credit score is calculated by your payment history, your credit utilization (the amount of credit you're using), the various types of credit you use, how long you've had credit, and inquiries made on your credit report. Credit scores range from 300-850 points.

CREDIT RATINGS:

Excellent Credit: 750 – 850

Good credit: 700 – 749

Fair Credit: 650 -699

Poor Credit: 600-649

Bad Credit: Below 600

A healthy credit score gives you more buying and negotiating power. It improves your chances of getting approved for apartments, gives you access to home and car loans, helps you avoid having to pay security deposits, and creates more investment opportunities.

MONITOR YOUR CREDIT REPORT

Businesses and banks check your credit report to decide whether or not to approve you for a credit card or loan. Property owners review your credit report to determine if they will rent you or not. Some employers even check your credit report as part of the application process. It's important to check your credit report at least once a year to make sure the information listed on it is correct.

Use Credit Karma to monitor your credit.

Credit Karma is a free online tool that offers scores, reports, and insights on your credit. Based on your credit report, Credit Karma makes suggestions on actions you can take to improve your credit score.

USE A SECURED CREDIT CARD TO INCREASE YOUR CREDIT SCORE

A secured credit card is a type of credit card that requires you to make a refundable deposit in exchange for a line of credit. Secured credit cards are ideal for building and repairing your credit because they don't require a good credit score to qualify.

Since secured credit cards report to the major credit bureaus, making on-time monthly payments will help improve your credit score.

Some secured credit cards place your deposit in a savings account that grows interest over time. Other secured credit cards have benefits such as low interest rates and rewards for making everyday purchases like buying groceries or gas.

USE A CREDIT BUILDER LOAN TO INCREASE YOUR CREDIT SCORE

A credit builder loan is one of the safest and easiest ways to improve your credit score. You simply make monthly payments into a secured savings account over the span of one or two years, and at the end of the year you receive the amount you paid in full.

Credit builder loans do not require a good credit score to qualify, and are ideal for building your credit.

Since credit builder loans report out to the major credit bureaus, making on-time monthly payments will help improve your credit score.

Credit builder loans are a great way to help you build healthy money habits while increasing your credit score.

ADDITIONAL TIPS
FOR GREAT CREDIT

---

1. Fix errors on your credit report. You can receive a free credit report every 12 months from each of the three major credit bureaus: Equifax, Experian, and TransUnion, using AnnualCreditReport.com.

2. Pay your credit card accounts down and don't use more than 30% of your overall credit limit.

3. Check your credit score frequently.

4. Do not co-sign on loans or credit cards that you can't afford to pay by yourself.

5. Avoid closing unused accounts. Closing unused accounts may decrease your overall credit limit and decrease your credit score. Keeping accounts open maintains your credit history.

6. Request a credit limit increase to lower your credit utilization and to increase your credit score.

7. Pay at *least* the minimum payment every month, and make multiple payments when you can.

8. Borrow as little as possible and *always* pay your credit card bills on time.

INVEST TO MAKE YOUR
MONEY GROW

If you want to achieve financial freedom, investing is the vehicle that will take you there. Investing is putting your money to work, allowing it to grow over time.

Investors can generate money by earning interest on the money they put aside, or by purchasing items that increase in value. Compound interest is a key component of investing. This is when the interest that you earn from the money you invest generates even more interest, making you more money.

Anyone can invest and thanks to technology, you can begin investing online and on your phone in a matter of minutes. You don't have to have a lot of money to begin investing. In fact, many investments can be started with under $5.

UNDERSTAND YOUR
INVESTMENT OPTIONS

Investment options are funds and accounts that can be used to grow your money over time. Using any of the following investment options is a great way to build wealth.

Stock: A share of ownership in a company. Owning a company's stock means that you own a percentage of the company and the company's profits.

Bond: A loan you make to an organization in exchange for interest payments over a certain amount of time.

Mutual Fund: An investment strategy that allows you to pool your money together with other people to purchase stocks, bonds, and other investments, while also earning interest. Mutual funds can only be bought and sold once a day.

Exchange-Traded Fund (ETF): Similar to a mutual fund, an ETF is an investment strategy that allows you to pool your money together to purchase stocks, bonds, and other investments, while also earning interest. ETFs can be traded multiple times throughout the day.

Retirement Account: Investments used when saving for retirement such as a 401(k), 403(b), or an Individual Retirement Account (IRA).

Annuity: An investment contract between you and an insurance company, promising to pay you for a specific amount of time.

Certificate of Deposit: A savings account that you agree to deposit money into for a set amount of time as it collects interest.

Life Insurance: An investment, often used for preserving wealth for generations, that pays out a sum of money, either on the death of the insured person, or after a set period.

Real Estate Investment Trust: A REIT is a corporation that owns and manages a portfolio of real estate properties. Anyone can buy shares in a REIT and own a portion of the real estate portfolio.

CREATE A RETIREMENT PLAN

TO INVEST FOR YOUR FUTURE

Having savings stashed away for retirement is the ultimate wealth-building strategy. Retirement accounts allow you to invest money for the future, while reaping the tax benefits now.

When it comes to retirement planning, time can be your greatest asset or your worst enemy. If you start early, time is on your side, and building wealth becomes easier. However, if you wait until retirement is just a few years away, it will become extremely difficult to catch up with saving, and you may be forced to live on a fixed income.

Although there are limits to the amount of money you can save each year, you are allowed to have more than one retirement account, setting you up for multiple streams of income for the future. Thanks to mobile apps and online resources, saving for retirement is now easier to do than ever before.

Use the retirement options on the next page to begin investing.

401(k): An employer-sponsored retirement plan that allows eligible employees to make tax-deductible contributions. This means you don't pay taxes until you withdraw your money. Employers may offer to match your contributions, giving you free money for retirement.

403(b): A retirement plan for employees of public schools and non-profit organizations. Similar to a 401(k), contributions are tax-deductible and employers may offer to match your contributions, giving you free money for retirement.

Traditional IRA: A Traditional Individual Retirement Account is a retirement plan that can be opened outside of your employer. Contributions are tax-deductible, and you only pay taxes when you withdraw your funds.

Roth IRA: A Roth IRA is a retirement plan that you pay taxes on upfront, so you aren't taxed on your money when it's distributed to you during retirement.

INVEST IN STOCK TO
GROW YOUR MONEY

Download the Acorns app to buy stock.

Acorns is a savings and investment mobile app that rounds every purchase you make to the nearest dollar, and then invests the difference. Acorns determines what kind of investments are best for you based on your income and financial goals, then gives you a plan to grow your money. Acorns is great for new investors who don't have much experience with choosing stock.

Download the Robinhood app to *trade* stock.

Robinhood is a stock trading mobile app that allows you to invest in the stock market without having to pay any trading fees. Robinhood gives you the option to choose the individual stocks you want to buy and trade to give you more control of your investments. The app is great for investors who have some knowledge of stock market trends and strategies.

BUILDING WEALTH IS A

MARATHON,

NOT A SPRINT.

GROWING YOUR MONEY TAKES

TIME, DISCIPLINE, AND DAILY ACTION.

THERE ARE NO LIMITS TO THE AMOUNT OF MONEY YOU CAN MAKE.

YOU MUST BELIEVE

YOU'RE WORTHY OF HAVING MONEY,

BELIEVE THAT IT'S POSSIBLE FOR YOU TO ACHIEVE

FINANCIAL FREEDOM, AND CONTINUE TO

BELIEVE IN YOURSELF,

BECAUSE YOU HAVE THE POWER TO

CREATE WEALTH AND LIVE ABUNDANTLY.

CHAPTER SEVEN

CROWN

YOUR PERSONAL POWER IS GREATER THAN ANY LIMITATION YOU WILL EVER FACE. THE KEY TO ACCESSING YOUR POWER IS TO HAVE CONFIDENCE IN YOURSELF AT ALL TIMES, AND ALWAYS REMEMBER THAT YOU CAN ACHIEVE ANYTHING.

#BELIEVEINYOURSELF

BELIEVING IN YOURSELF

IS THE HARDEST THING YOU'LL EVER HAVE TO DO,

BECAUSE THERE ARE SO MANY REMINDERS

WHY YOU *SHOULDN'T* DO IT.

YOUR

INNER CRITIC

WILL TRY TO DISCOURAGE YOU FROM
WORKING ON YOUR DREAMS:

"YOU'RE TOO YOUNG."
"YOU'RE NOT EXPERIENCED."
"YOU DON'T HAVE THE SKILLS."
"YOU DON'T HAVE THE EDUCATION."
"YOU DON'T HAVE THE MONEY."
"YOUR PLAN WILL NEVER WORK."

PEOPLE WILL

CRITICIZE YOU,

MANY WILL

DOUBT YOU.

THE ONES CLOSEST TO YOU WILL TRY TO DISTRACT YOU
FROM YOUR GOALS. FAMILY WILL TRY TO CONVINCE
YOU THAT YOUR DREAM IS ONLY A FANTASY.
FRIENDS WILL REMIND YOU OF YOUR
FAILURES AND SHORTCOMINGS.

OBSTACLES WILL TRY TO SLOW YOU DOWN AND TRICK
YOU INTO BELIEVING THAT YOU CAN'T ACHIEVE THE
SUCCESS YOU DESERVE.

IN

THE

PROCESS

OF WORKING

ON YOUR DREAMS

YOU'LL EXPERIENCE SETBACKS,

CHALLENGES, DIFFICULTIES, AND DEFEAT.

IT WON'T

BE EASY.

BUT AS YOU

CONTINUE

TO DEVELOP

YOURSELF,

YOU WILL

SEE THAT

YOU ARE

STRONGER

THAN YOU

THINK, AND

GREATER

THAN YOU

COULD EVER

IMAGINE.

YOUR

CROWN

IS YOUR CONFIDENCE.

IT REPRESENTS YOUR AMBITION AND DETERMINATION.
IT'S YOUR ABILITY TO TAKE ACTION AND REMOVE EVERY
LIMITATION. IT SYMBOLIZES PERSEVERANCE DESPITE THE
PAIN THAT YOU'VE BEEN THROUGH. IT REPRESENTS
WHAT YOU WORK FOR, AND FORESHADOWS
THE GREAT THINGS YOU *WILL* DO.

IT'S THE FOUNDATION FOR
ABUNDANCE AND GENERATIONAL WEALTH.
IT'S YOUR WISDOM, YOUR UNDERSTANDING,
AND YOUR KNOWLEDGE OF SELF.

YOUR CROWN IS THE KEY TO DEFEATING YOUR INNER
CRITIC, AND SILENCING SELF-DEFEATING THOUGHTS
WHILE REMAINING OPTIMISTIC.

YOUR DESTINY IS DETERMINED BY YOUR CHOICES AND
DECISIONS; NOT YOUR ENVIRONMENT, NOT YOUR
CONDITIONS. IT'S NOT DETERMINED BY YOUR PAST, YOUR
SHORTCOMINGS OR OBSTACLES. YOUR CROWN IS A
REMINDER THAT NOTHING IS *EVER* IMPOSSIBLE.

IT'S POSSIBLE

FOR YOU TO GET THAT PROMOTION.

IT'S POSSIBLE

FOR YOU TO BUY THAT HOUSE.

IT'S POSSIBLE

FOR YOU TO WRITE YOUR BOOK.

IT'S POSSIBLE

FOR YOU TO START YOUR BUSINESS.

IT'S POSSIBLE

FOR YOU TO BECOME WEALTHY,

TO TRAVEL THE WORLD, TO PURSUE YOUR DREAM,

TO LIVE ABUNDANTLY, AND TO ACHIEVE

MASSIVE SUCCESS.

BY LEARNING ABOUT YOURSELF, DEVELOPING YOURSELF,

AND REINVENTING YOURSELF, YOUR CONFIDENCE WILL

INCREASE, YOUR OPPORTUNITIES WILL MULTIPLY,

AND YOU _WILL_ ACHIEVE SUCCESS.

DEFINE YOUR DREAM,

COMMIT TO KNOWING YOURSELF,

BE DISCIPLINED

WHEN WORKING ON YOUR GOALS,

TAKE ACTION, EMBRACE CHALLENGES,

LEARN FROM FAILURES,

JUMP OVER BARRIERS,

ELIMINATE LIMITATIONS, AVOID DISTRACTIONS

PREPARE FOR ABUNDANCE,

PERSEVERE UNTIL YOU

REACH SUCCESS,

AND ABOVE ALL...

BELIEVE IN YOURSELF.

ABOUT THE AUTHOR

Marques Clark is an educator and social entrepreneur with a passion for helping others become the best version of themselves. After completing his Master of Science in Education, Marques went on to start ClarkHouse, LLC, a publishing company that combines pop culture and education to teach, train, and engage. Through books, workshops, and curriculum development, Marques helps businesses and schools connect with young audiences using pop culture.

Marques is a board member of The Urban Male Network, Inc., a non-profit organization that empowers young men to become leaders through mentorship, community development, and the promotion of a positive image. He lives in Illinois with his wife, Kyndall, and their two sons, Micah and Noah.

ACKNOWLEDGEMENTS

To the 100+ men who dedicated their time, shared their strategies, and revealed their secrets, THANK YOU. There is no possible way this book would exist without your help and transparency. It is an honor and a blessing to have the opportunity to interview such phenomenal people.

Contributors – Thank you Quincy A. Bevely, John Bodie, Randy C. Bonds, André T. Clark, Paul L. Collins, Derrick M. Flemming, Jr., Willis E. Harper Jr., Dr. Marlon Haywood, Randiss Hopkins, George Jideonwo, James Johnson, Isaiah Mākar, Sedrick McDonald, Steven L. McDonald, Jr., Alandis R. Phillips, and Stephen Samuels for sharing your intelligence, motivation, advice, and for helping me articulate my thoughts. I am humbly grateful for each and every one of you.

Models – Thank you Randy C. Bonds, Adam Collins, Dr. Marlon Haywood, Robert I. Hunley III, Isaiah Mākar, Brandon Marshall, Dezmond Mayfield, Kendall Robinson, Stephen Samuels for allowing me to use your modeling skills to make this book possible.

Finally, thank you to my parents, my friends, my extended family, my wife, Kyndall, and my sons, Micah and Noah. I am forever grateful for your constant love and support.

THANK YOU

THANK YOU for reading REINVENTION. If you enjoyed this book, please take a minute to visit the site where you purchased it and write a brief review. Your feedback is extremely important to me and it will help other readers make the decision to read the book.

If you'd like to order copies of this book for your company, school, or group of friends, please email me at mclark@clarkhousepublishing.com.

Finally, if you'd like receive updates on my future projects, please visit my blog at www.morepopculture.com.

NOTES

CONTENT FROM REINVENTION WAS INSPIRED BY BIBLICAL SPRICTURE. EXCERPTS BELOW ARE TAKEN FROM THE WORLD ENGLIGH BIBLE (WEB).

1. **CHAPTER 1: MIRRORS (SELF-AWARENESS) – Romans 12:2**

   "Do not be conformed to this world, but be transformed by the renewing of your mind, so that you may prove what is the good, well-pleasing, and perfect will of God."

2. **CHAPTER 2: STORMS (RESILIENCE) – 1 Corinthians 10:13**

   "No temptation has taken you except what is common to man. God is faithful, who will not allow you to be tempted above what you are able, but will with the temptation also make the way of escape, that you may be able to endure it."

3. **CHAPTER 3: LUXURY (GRATITUDE) – Philippians 4:6**

   "In nothing be anxious, but in everything, by prayer and petition with thanksgiving, let your requests be made known to God."

4. **CHAPTER 4: LIMITLESS (SUCCESS HABITS) – Proverbs 16:3**

   "Commit your deeds to Yahweh and your plans shall succeed."

5. **CHAPTER 5: POWER (POWER CIRCLE) – Proverbs 13:20**

   "One who walks with wise men grows wise, but a companion of fools suffers harm."

6. **CHAPTER 6: MA$TERMIND (FINANCIAL LITERACY) – Proverbs 21:5**

   "The plans of the diligent surely lead to profit; and everyone who is hasty surely rushes to poverty."

7. **CHAPTER 7: CROWN (CONFIDENCE) – JAMES 1:12**

   "Blessed is a person who endures temptation, for when he has been approved, he will receive the crown of life, which the Lord promised to those who love him."

Printed in Great Britain
by Amazon